Commissioned by Worthing Choral Society, conductor Aedan Kerney,
and first performed on 15 November 2014 at
St George's Church, St George's Road, Worthing, West Su

A Winter's Night

Christmas Cantata

for SATB, brass quintet, percussion and or

1. In Dulci Jubilo

German, 14th cent.
Translation: R.L. Pearsall

CECILIA McDOWALL

Our de-light and plea-sure Lies *in prae-se-pi - o* Like sun-shine is our trea - sure Ma -
Un-sers Her-zens Won - ne Leit Und leuch-tet als die Son - ne

Our de-light and plea-sure Lies *in prae-se-pi - o* Like sun-shine is our trea - sure Ma -
Un-sers Her-zens Won - ne Leit Und leuch-tet als die Son - ne

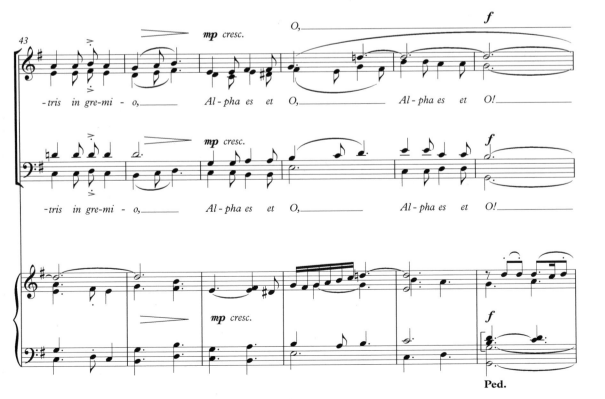

-tris in gre-mi - o, Al - pha es et O, O, Al - pha es et O!

-tris in gre-mi - o, Al - pha es et O, Al - pha es et O!

Ped.

4

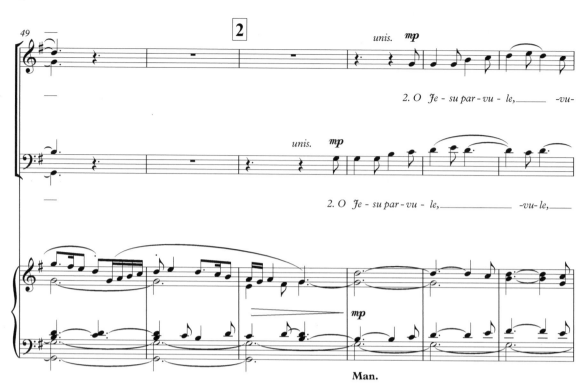

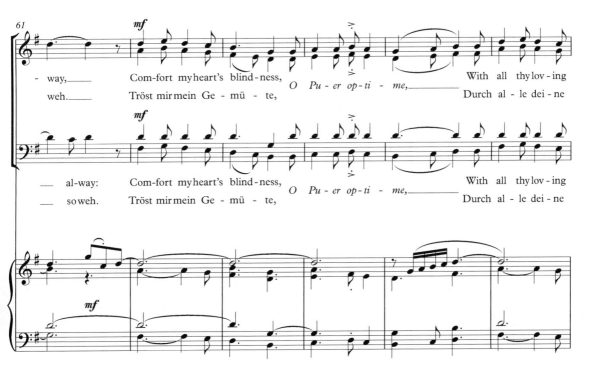

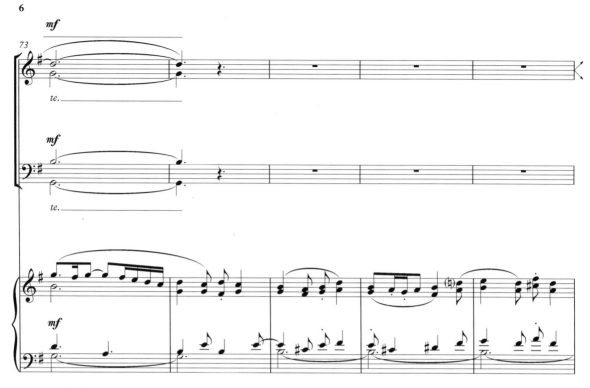

(Man.)

8

2. O little one sweet

Translation: Percy Dearmer

17th-century German melody

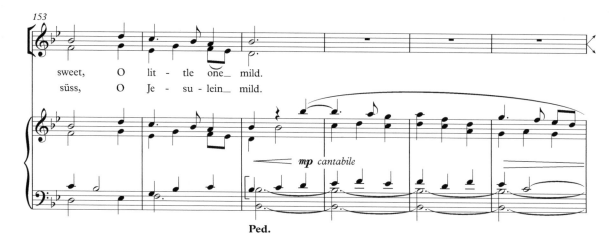

201

sweet,   O   lit – tle one   mild.
süss,   O   Je – su-lein   mild.

sweet,   O   lit – tle   one_   mild.
süss,   O   Je – su – lein_   mild.

sweet,   O   lit – tle   one   mild.
süss,_   O   Je – su – lein   mild.

sweet,   O   lit – tle   one   mild.
süss,   O   Je – su – lein   mild.

mp cresc.

Ped.

3. Noël Nouvelet

French Traditional, 15th cent.

ad lib.

Bright, rhythmic ♩ = 92 (♪ = ♪ sempre)

8

f marcato ma leggiero

Man.

207

211

18

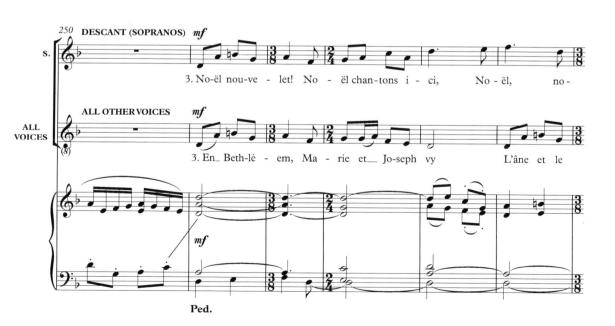

11

-ël, l'En - fant cou - ché par - mi; La crêche é - tait au lieu d'un ber - ce-

boeuf, l'En - fant cou - ché par - mi; La crêche é - tait au lieu d'un ber - ce-

- let,___ No - ël___ nou - ve - let! No - ël chan - tons i - ci.

- let,___ No - ël nou - ve - let! No - ël chan - tons i - ci.

Man. Ped.

SOPRANOS & ALTOS

S.
A.

4. Bien - tôt les rois, par l'é - toile é - clair-

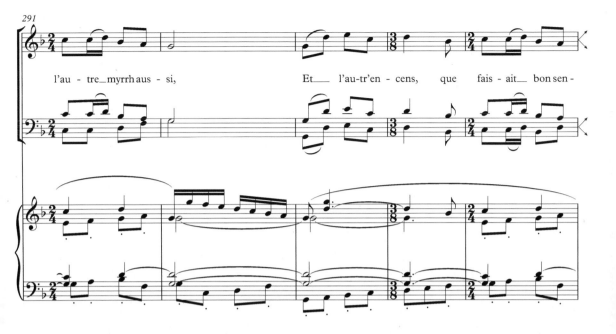

22

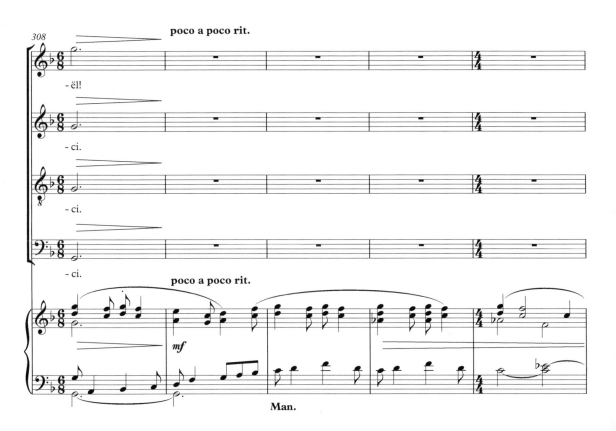

4. Still, still, still

Austrian carol (1819)
Translation: Angier Brock

13 SOPRANOS (or SOPRANO solo)

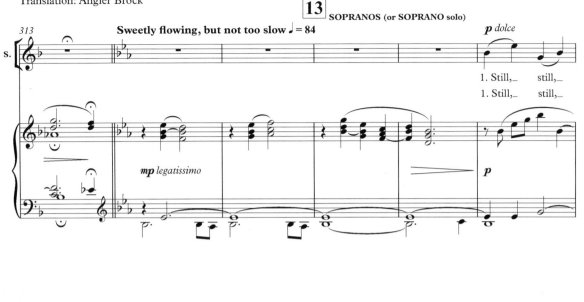

14

26

28

Man.   Ped.

17

5. Sussex Carol

Traditional English, 17th cent.

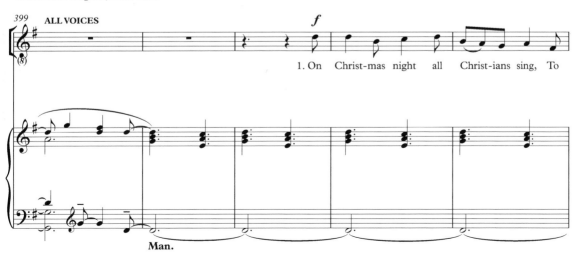

ALL VOICES

1. On Christ-mas night all Christ-ians sing, To

Man.

32

19

3.When sin de-parts be - fore his grace, Then life and health come

in its place, When sin de-parts be - fore his grace, Then life and health come

in its place; An - gels and men with joy may sing, All for to

(TENORS & BASSES) An - gels and men with joy may sing, All for to

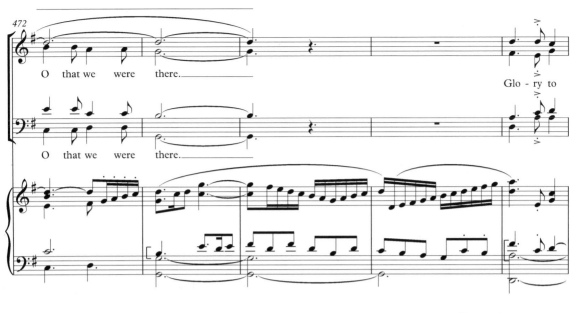